Holidays Around the World

T0011436

Celebrate Kwanzaa

Carolyn Otto
Consultant, Keith A. Mayes, Ph.D.

NATIONAL GEOGRAPHIC
WASHINGTON, D.C.

candles

^ A kinara

We celebrate Kwanzaa from December 26 through January 1. Each day we join our friends and families to light a special candle. We think about what it means to be part of the black community, in America and in the world. We celebrate our ancestry.

community

< *A young girl leaps into joyous dance in celebration of Kwanzaa at the American Museum of Natural History in New York City.*

^ *The Jeter family*

ancestry

Kwanzaa was created in 1966

during the black power movement to honor African-American people, our struggles in the United States, our heritage, and our culture. The name Kwanzaa means "first fruits" of the harvest.

During Kwanzaa, we gather together to give thanks for the harvest, which brings us the good things of the earth. We remember the past and our ancestors, who worked the earth. We celebrate hope and promise for the year to come.

> *In the Ethiopian Highlands, a girl carries a bundle of wheat.*

We celebrate
the harvest.

We say, "Jambo!"

A Masaii warrior in the East African country of Kenya

Africa is a big continent.

It has many countries, many people, and many different languages. The words we use to celebrate Kwanzaa come from the Swahili language. Swahili is spoken mostly in East and Central Africa, but you can hear it in places all over the world.

About 35 million people speak Swahili. If you wanted to greet someone in that language, you would say, "Jambo!"

"Hello!"

^ *A U.S. postage stamp commemorates Kwanzaa.*

Before the celebration begins, we decorate our homes with the colors and symbols of Kwanzaa. The colors are red, green, and black. We use wall hangings, African cloth, and special artwork.

We make beautiful

things for Kwanzaa.

∧ *In a California classroom, children weave strips of paper into* mkeka *mats.*

< *Marjorie Terrell displays dolls dressed with lovely African cloth in Plainfield, New Jersey.*

We can buy decorations, but it's more fun to make them ourselves. Creativity is one of the seven principles of Kwanzaa, so we use our imaginations.

In our decorations, we include

many important symbols of Kwanzaa. We put a mat, called an *mkeka,* on our tables. We arrange a basket filled with fruits and vegetables on the mkeka, to represent the harvest. Ears of corn are placed on the mat, one for each child in the family. The *kikombe cha umoja,* or unity cup, is placed there, too.

v *In Oakland, California, a boy places a lighted candle in a kinara.*

mkeka

Most important is the *kinara,* the special candleholder, and the seven candles it holds—one black, three red, and three green.

kikombe cha umoja

kinara

^ *A father holds his daughter, who in turn holds the unity cup. It is usually filled with water—something pure from the earth.*

> *A woman celebrates Kwanzaa at home.*

We can't wait
for Kwanzaa!

> A gourd rattle

As Kwanzaa gets closer,

we practice drumming and dancing. We buy or make gifts, called *zawadi,* for our friends and families. We help others make gifts, too. A parent, an older brother or sister, or a friend might show younger children how to make drums and rattles and rainsticks, colored necklaces, or woven mats.

Gifts can be given any time during the week of Kwanzaa, but mostly we wait until the last day. It's not easy to be patient.

< *In Florida, Paige Armour shrieks with laughter when a present is "stolen" from her by her friend, Gloria Dover. Swapping food and gifts is a traditional game in many parts of Africa.*

On the 26th of December, we light the first candle of Kwanzaa. It is the center, black candle. The black candle stands for the unity of black people. Unity means standing together and helping each other.

Over the next six days we will light six more candles—three red and three green—one each day. The red candles on the left side represent our past. We remember our ancestors, many of whom were brought to this country as slaves. We think of their struggles and their triumphs. The green candles on the right stand for our hopes and dreams for the future.

> *Travis Holley lights the first candle of this Kwanzaa celebration in Linden, New Jersey.*

We celebrate
with candles.

A family in South Pasadena, California, reads together during Kwanzaa.

Each day we light another candle.

We talk about the seven principles of Kwanzaa:

UMOJA (unity): Striving for togetherness with our families and communities.

KUJICHAGULIA (self-determination): Deciding for ourselves who we are, who we want to be, and what we want to do.

UJIMA (work and responsibility): Working together to build and strengthen our communities.

The seven principles

UJAMAA (cooperation): Building and supporting African-American stores and businesses and benefiting from them together.

NIA (purpose): Setting personal goals to make our communities strong.

KUUMBA (creativity): Thinking of ways to make our community and the world a better place.

IMANI (faith): Believing in ourselves, our communities, and the people around us.

^ *A mancala board*

We gather together to sing, dance, play drums, and celebrate our culture. Sometimes we play games. Grown-ups and children like to play *mancala,* a board game that is popular around the world. It is played with pebbles, beads, or seeds and can be played almost anywhere.

We gather together.

∧ *In New York City, people join hands in celebration of community and unity.*

< *Four children play mancala in East Africa.*

During Kwanzaa, we eat special foods. Some families use recipes passed from one generation to the next. We might have peanut soup or shrimp gumbo. Sometimes we have fried bananas, sweet potato pie, or coconut sweets.

fun

^ *African-American children perform a folk dance in the Bronx, New York.*

friends

On the sixth day or night of the holiday, we have a great feast, called the Karamu. We dress in bright clothing to display the patterns and colors of Africa. We have drumming, music, and dance. We sing. We welcome as many people as we can. And we eat!

< *Young men drum for the Kwanzaa feast of Karamu, which celebrates creativity. Drumming is a form of communication as well as celebration.*

feast

January 1 is the last day of Kwanzaa. It is a quieter time. We have a farewell ceremony for Kwanzaa. We greet the new year. We focus on the things we have learned. We give one another gifts. We remember our roots and the traditions of our ancestors. We think of their struggles, and we

A girl in Washington, D.C., waits for her turn to dance in celebration of Kwanzaa.

our roots.

We wish for strength.

We wish to be united as one people and to work together to make the world better for those to come. We hope to preserve the good things in our lives and in our world.

We hope to make the world a better place.

> *In New York City, members of a dance company perform a traditional African dance.*

MORE ABOUT KWANZAA

Contents

Just the Facts 26
Slavery 26
Make a Rainstick 27
Sweet Potato Pie 28
Find Out More 29
Glossary 30
Map of Photograph Locations 30
Kwanzaa: An African-American Holiday With Universal Appeal 31

Just the Facts

WHO CELEBRATES IT: African Americans and their friends and families.

WHAT: A holiday to celebrate African-American heritage, culture, achievements, and future.

WHEN: December 26 through January 1.

RITUAL: Lighting a candle each day, remembering the past, and celebrating the future. Drumming, dancing, making and giving gifts, feasting.

FOOD: A feast to celebrate harvest time. It includes everything from coconut milk and banana fritters to collard greens and sweet potato dishes.

Slavery

Most Africans were forced to come to America against their will. They came as slaves. Slaves were bought and sold. They were treated like possessions. Families were broken. People lived their whole lives without hope of freedom for themselves or their children.

Kwanzaa celebrates the need to know about the past and to create a more positive future. After the years of slavery, segregation, and the struggle for civil rights and justice, black people in the United States wanted to rediscover their roots and take pride in their African ancestry.

Kwanzaa celebrates the black community and the unity and triumph of black people.

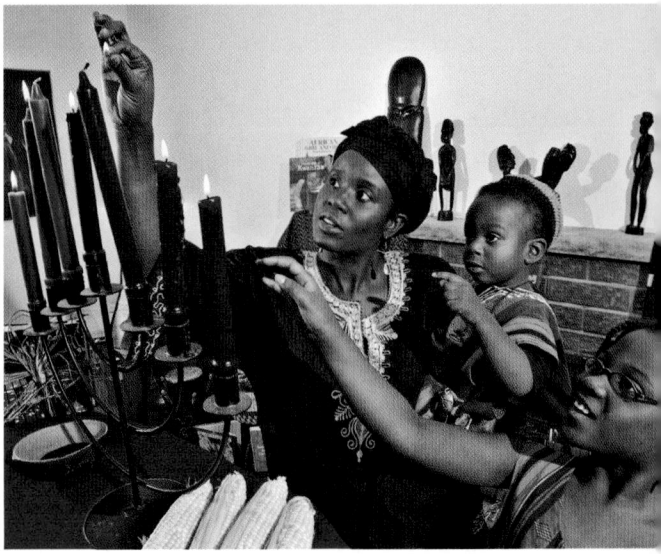

> *A woman lights candles for Kwanzaa with her children in Toronto, Canada.*

< *A rainstick displays the rich decorations of Africa.*

Make a Rainstick

Clank clink, tap tap, shushhhh . . . These are some of the sounds you might hear from rainsticks and rattles during a Kwanzaa music and dance celebration. You can make very different sounds with them, depending on the container you use and what you put in it. Small dried pasta makes a *rat-a-tat-tat* sound, dried beans go *tap tap tap*, and rice makes a sort of *shushhhh*. You can use any kind of cardboard tube. Be creative!

YOU WILL NEED:

A cardboard tube (wrapping paper tubes are perfect!)
Waxed paper
Rubber bands
Grains of rice, pasta, or dried beans
Pushpin

1

Decorate the empty tube with African colors (red, green, and black), stickers, pictures, glitter—whatever you want.

2

Cover one end of the tube with waxed paper and attach the paper tightly with a rubber band.

3

Pour a handful of dried beans, rice, or pasta into the open end. Seal the opening with waxed paper and a rubber band.

4

Poke holes in the tube with the pushpin. Turn the tube very slowly or shake it quickly and listen to the different sounds you can make.

A piece of sweet potato pie, creamy and delicious.

Sweet Potato Pie

Recipes like this one for sweet potato pie are often handed down from one generation to the next. This family favorite is sweet and delicious. Be sure to have an adult help you at the stove.

INGREDIENTS:

2 large eggs
1/2 cup plus 2 tablespoons sugar
dash salt
1/2 teaspoon cinnamon
1/4 teaspoon allspice
1/8 teaspoon nutmeg
1/4 teaspoon lemon juice
1/2 teaspoon vanilla
1/2 cup heavy cream
1 1/2 cups cooked, mashed sweet potatoes
1 unbaked pie shell

1. Preheat oven to 350°F.
2. Beat eggs well. Add sugar, salt, spices, lemon juice, and vanilla to the eggs. Mix thoroughly.
3. Add cream and stir.
4. Add mashed sweet potatoes and mix thoroughly.
5. Turn into pie shell and bake for 1 hour or until firm.
6. Let pie cool. Serve warm or cold.

Find Out More

BOOKS

Those with a star (*) are especially good for children.

***Brady, April A. *Kwanzaa Karamu: Cooking and Crafts for a Kwanzaa Feast.* Carolrhoda Books, 1995.** Explains the origins of the holiday and provides recipes and crafts.

Grier, Ella. *Seven Days of Kwanzaa: How to Celebrate Them.* Sterling, 2005. A good overview of the Kwanzaa celebration day by day. Illustrated by John Ward.

Karenga, Maulana. *Kwanzaa: A Celebration of Family, Community, and Culture.* University of Sankore Press, 1997. By the creator of Kwanzaa.

***Marsh, Carole. *Kwanzaa: Activities, Crafts, Recipes, and More!* Gallopade International, 2003.** Great for kids of all ages.

***Medearis, Angela Shelf. *Seven Spools of Thread: A Kwanzaa Story.* Albert Whitman and Company, 2000.** A beautiful tale of seven brothers who overcome their differences. Illustrated with woodcuts by Daniel Minter.

***Morninghouse, Sundaira. *Habari Gani? What's the News?: A Kwanzaa Story.* Open Hand Publishers, 1992.** An engagingly illustrated book to share with younger children. Illustrated by Jody Kim.

WEBSITES

A note for parents and teachers: For more information on this topic, you can visit these websites with your young readers.

childfun.com
For facts, crafts, and recipes, go to "Holidays" in the site menu and click on "Winter Holidays," then "Kwanzaa Themed Activities."

familyeducation.com
Type in "Kwanzaa" as the key word in the search engine, and follow the links for information and fun.

EDUCATIONAL EXTENSIONS

Reading

1. According to tradition, people often hand-make decorations and *zawadi* (gifts) as they celebrate Kwanzaa. Why is this an important aspect of the holiday season?
2. Can you explain the significance of the kinara during Kwanzaa? How does it help people remember the past as well as celebrate the future?
3. Pick a favorite photograph from the book and reread its caption. What symbols of Kwanzaa can you see in the details of the image? (Hint: Expand upon the information given in the caption and the details you observe visually in relation to the context of the page.)

v Harold Anderson (left) and Jose Ferrer unveil the first Kwanzaa postage stamp in 1997, in Harlem, New York City.

Glossary

Ancestry: Your family's background and history.

Imani (ee-MAH-nee): Faith.

Karamu (Ka-RAH-moo): A feast held on the seventh day of Kwanzaa.

Kikombe cha umoja (kee-KOHM-bee chah oo-MO-jah): The unity cup, which is passed from person to person during Kwanzaa.

Kinara (kee-NAH-rah): A candleholder for the seven candles of Kwanzaa.

Kujichagulia (koo-jee-chah-GOO-lee-ah): Self-determination.

Kuumba (koo-OOM-bah): Creativity.

Mkeka (em-KEH-kah): A mat or table covering.

Nguzo Saba (n-GU-zo SAH-bah): The seven principles of Kwanzaa.

Nia (NEE-ah): Purpose.

Ujamaa (oo-jah-MAH-ah): Cooperative economics.

Ujima (oo-JEE-mah): Collective work and responsibility.

Umoja (oo-MO-jah): Unity.

Where This Book's Photos Were Taken

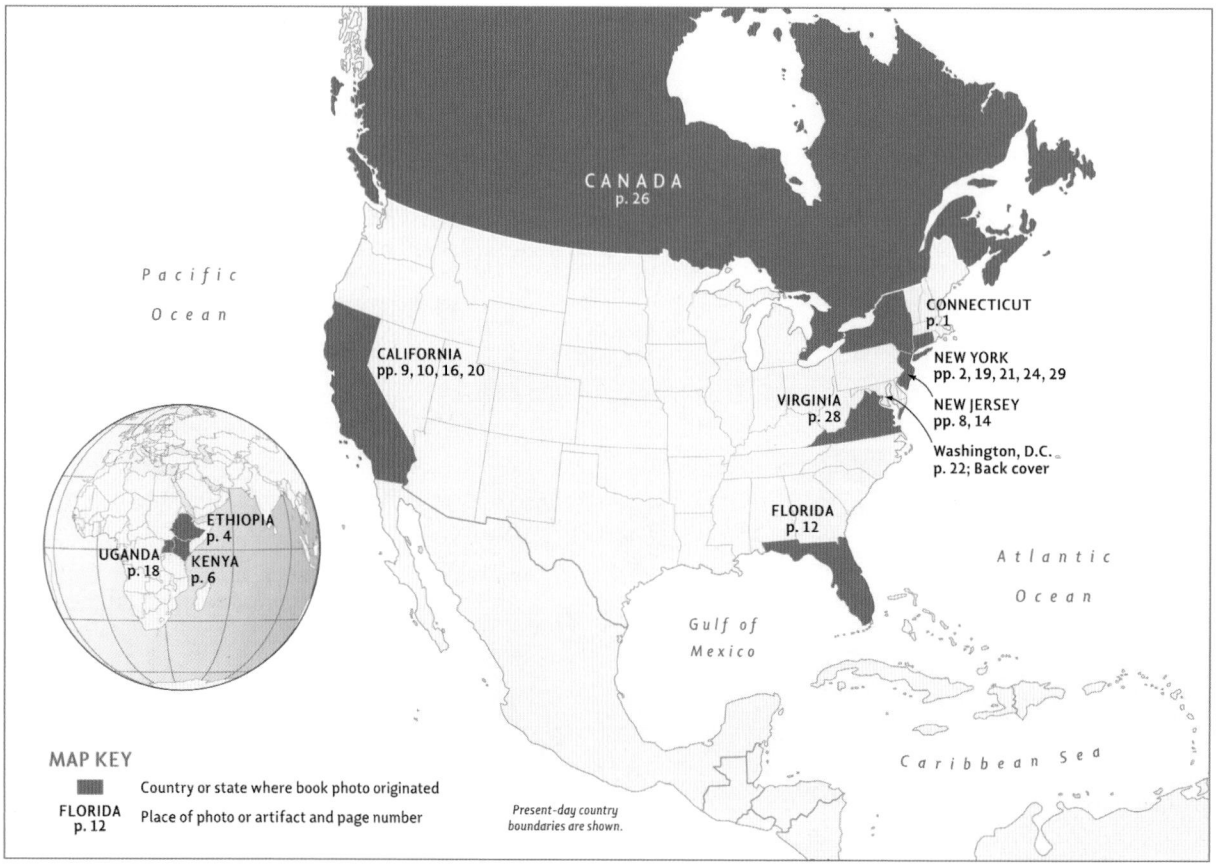

Kwanzaa: An African-American Holiday With Universal Appeal

by Keith A. Mayes, Ph.D.

Although Kwanzaa is not an African holiday, it was inspired by African culture and is based on African cultural practices. Kwanzaa was created in 1966 by Maulana Karenga and the Us organization in Los Angeles during the civil rights and black power movements that began in the 1950s and continued through the 1970s. The civil rights movement sought to eliminate segregation and discrimination in areas such as public accommodations, education, housing, and employment.

The black power movement, however, focused on the African-American quest for self-discovery and group identity. Searching for this identity from a new understanding of what it meant to be African and finding pride in blackness became its major preoccupation. Whereas civil rights is associated with the South, nonviolent direct action, and the strategies employed by Martin Luther King, Jr., black power highlighted an African past and an existence that transcended U.S. boundaries.

Kwanzaa is a prime example of African Americans' desire to discover their African heritage and reconnect with the continent of their ancestors. In fact, Kwanzaa is the product not of one individual but of an entire community. Kwanzaa would not be known to the world today if it were not for the black community in the late 1960s and early 1970s. In cities across the U.S., black social activists as well as apolitical African Americans embraced Kwanzaa and promoted the holiday in their homes, schools, and community centers.

Today, young people may be Kwanzaa's largest audience and most important constituents. Many black children have been introduced to Kwanzaa in their homes or schools, where the African side of African-American identity has been reinforced. Kwanzaa has rooted African-American children in their history and culture, providing them with a sense of belonging in the world. This sense of belonging not only means that black children have a holiday of their own, it also reinforces the idea that African Americans come from a people that have made significant contributions to human history and possess a glorious past. Kwanzaa's appeal to young people has much to do with posterity. Young people represent the future—their own future and the future of those not yet born. Not only are black youth heirs and custodians of Kwanzaa who can ensure the holiday's survival, but they are also the heirs and custodians of a brighter future for African Americans in general. This is what Kwanzaa speaks to.

Although Kwanzaa is grounded in black culture, the holiday's seven principles represent universal values that anyone can relate to. The principles of unity, self-determination, collective work and responsibility, cooperative economics, purpose, creativity, and faith are not "black" values—they are universal. Kwanzaa has transcended the boundaries of black America. The holiday is recognized by mainstream American society, and celebrations are held in major museums, libraries, and religious institutions across the U.S. and around the world.

Kwanzaa's growth and appeal beyond black America reflects the universality of its main components and symbols. Like other holidays, Kwanzaa is values oriented and driven, historically rooted, activities based, and youth focused—giving it a universal appeal. In this sense, the holiday represents the best of African-American culture, U.S. society, and humanity: unique, experimental, creative, improvisational, and put together from many parts.

Consultant Keith Mayes is an assistant professor in the Department of African-American and African Studies at the University of Minnesota. His writings include "Kwanzaa and the African-American Holiday Tradition" in American Holidays and National Days, *edited by Len Travers.*

For Renee

PICTURE CREDITS

Cover, Mark Adams/Taxi/Getty Images; back cover, Brendan Smialowski/AFP/Getty Images; spine (fabric), Comstock; (kinara), Brock Meeler/iStockphoto; 1, Arnold Gold/New Haven Register/The Image Works; 2, Mario Tama/Getty Images; 3 (UP), Hill Street Studios/Blend Images/Corbis; 3 (LO), The New York Public Library; 4-5, Gavin Hellier/Robert Harding World Imagery/Getty Images; 6-7, John Warburton-Lee Photography; 8 (UP), USPS/Associated Press; 8 (LO), Frank Conlon/The Star-Ledger/Corbis; 9, Contra Costa Newspapers/Kristopher Skinner/ZUMA Press; 10, Lonny Shavelson/ZUMA Press; 11 (UP), Tom Wilson/Taxi/Getty Images; 11 (LO), Photo Network/Alamy Ltd; 12-13, Amanda Voisard/Palm Beach Post/ZUMA Press; 13, Comstock; 14-15, Tim Farrell/The Star-Ledger/Corbis; 16, FoodPix/Jupiter Images; 18 (UP), Kenneth Sponsler/Shutterstock; 18 (LO), Bea Ahbeck/Fremont Argus/ZUMA Press; 19, Jennifer Szymaszek/Associated Press; 20, Kayte M. Deioma/PhotoEdit Inc.; 21, James Leynse/Corbis/Getty Images; 22-23, Brendan Smialowski/AFP/Getty Images; 24-25, Stephen Chernin/Getty Images; 26, David Cooper/Toronto Star/ZUMA Press; 27, Sébastien Fortier/iStockphoto; 28, Mary Beth Keegan; 29, Bebeto Matthews/Associated Press

Published by National Geographic Partners, LLC.

Text copyright © 2008 Carolyn Otto
Compilation copyright © 2008 National Geographic Society
Reprinted in paperback and library binding, 2017

All rights reserved. Reproduction of the whole or any part of the contents without written permission from the publisher is prohibited.

The Library of Congress cataloged the 2008 edition as follows:
Otto, Carolyn.
Celebrate Kwanzaa / Carolyn Otto; consultant, Keith A. Mayes.
p. cm. —(Holidays around the world)
ISBN 978-1-4263-0319-7 (trade) — ISBN 978-1-4263-0320-3 (library)
1. Kwanzaa—Juvenile literature. 2. United States—Social life and customs—Juvenile literature. I. Title. GT4403.O88 2007
394.2612—dc22
2007041221

2017 paperback edition ISBN: 978-1-4263-2849-7
2017 reinforced library binding ISBN: 978-1-4263-2850-3

Series design by 3+Co. and Jim Hiscott.
The body text in the book is set in Mrs. Eaves.
The display text is Lisboa.

Front cover: These parents are teaching their daughter what the kinara candles stand for.
Back cover: A fully lit kinara rests among some symbols of Kwanzaa.
Title page: A boy lights the candles during Kwanzaa.

NATIONAL GEOGRAPHIC and Yellow Border Design are trademarks of the National Geographic Society, used under license.

Since 1888, the National Geographic Society has funded more than 14,000 research, conservation, education, and storytelling projects around the world. National Geographic Partners distributes a portion of the funds it receives from your purchase to National Geographic Society to support programs including the conservation of animals and their habitats. To learn more, visit natgeo.com/info.

For more information, visit nationalgeographic.com, call 1-877-873-6846, or write to the following address:

National Geographic Partners, LLC
1145 17th Street NW
Washington, DC 20036-4688 U.S.A.

For librarians and teachers:
nationalgeographic.com/books/librarians-and-educators

More for kids from National Geographic: natgeokids.com

For rights or permissions inquiries, please contact National Geographic Books Subsidiary Rights: bookrights@natgeo.com

The publisher would like to thank Kelsey Carlson, education consultant.

Printed in the United States of America
22/WOR/4

ACKNOWLEDGMENTS

Many thanks to Dr. Keith Mayes for his insightful editorial comments and powerful note. To Tammi Hawes, another teacher whose influence upon our children is profound. And to Nancy, Mary Beth, and Amy, for helping me get things right.